To Tim a
fellow writ



# Rimes of Ancient Fables

# Rimes of Ancient Fables

Illustrated by Gina Haver

Carl J. Hasper

ProPress Books, Inc.
Massapequa, New York

ProPress Books, Inc.
Massapequa, New York
www.propressbooks.net

ISBN 978-0-9915627-0-1
PRINTED IN THE UNITED STATES OF AMERICA

# Dedication

This book is dedicated to Barbara, my wife of over fifty-five years. She cooked, did the laundry, tended our house, was a good mother for our daughter Marianne, and also had a career as a High School mathematics teacher for thirty-four years. She loves the beauty of nature.

Her unwavering goodness in taking care of her mother, Marion, for sixteen years, in spite of difficulties, and empathy for stray cats, and tolerance for me, a feral human, has ensnared us all in a cocoon bonded by silken threads of love.

It is also dedicated to our daughter Marianne and her husband Stephan, our best friends and formidable opponents in our weekly games.

# *Table of Contents*

# Acknowledgements

This book would not have been written if not for the assistance of others, who have motivated the author. My wife Barbara had urged me to publish what I have written so others can enjoy it.

Dr. George Dawson praised my early efforts to write poetry. He told me "Your poetry is darn good." Professor Dawson, a poet himself, was not tall in physical height, but tall in moral and intellectual stature. He was the author or co-author of many economics textbooks, the editor of magazines, the chairman of the economics department at NYU, a US Navy veteran of WWII and the Korean War, and leader of the first US Peace Corps contingent in Somalia, and also a good drummer in a band. He thought the Somali people were possibly the world's best poets, in spite of being mostly illiterate. Our nation lost an inspiring citizen when he died earlier this year. I'll never forget him.

Mary Haughey, whose creative writing classes I've attended for the last several years, has a talent for teasing out a desire to write and building confidence in her students. They are wonderful writers. Many of them have been published in newspapers, magazines and books. They have been kind to me by applauding my writing. We are like a family.

Grace Zolla Protano, the publisher, has been helpful and kind and patient.

Gina Haver brought the fables to life with her charming illustrations. She is not only a wonderful artist, but also an accomplished opera singer.

Lorraine Conlin, of the Performance Poets Association, is the Poet Laureate of Nassau County. She hosts poetic events several times a week at locations sprinkled all over the map of Long Island, and has been kind enough to invite us to them, and there is usually an open mike.

— Carl J. Hasper

# Foreword

Carl Hasper, author of *Rimes of Ancient Fables*, is my husband. He was an Electrical Engineer and not interested in liberal arts until several years after he retired.

Writing rhymed poetry has become his passion. He wants to use his poetry to entertain and also teach. It's a "Double Whammy."

— Barbara Hasper

# Preface

Since retirement about twenty years ago, I have acquired a passion for writing rhymed poetry. I'm a member of various local writing groups and my fellow writers have made favorable comments about the poems.

I'm an amateur poet, and as an exercise to practice writing poetry, I re-write Aesop's fables in my own words as prose, and then as rhymed couplets of ten syllables per line. It is fun. I hope to publish the hundreds of other poems I have written in future books.

— Carl J. Hasper

# Aesop

Aesop was born about 620 BC, but no one knows exactly when, or where. He was the slave of Iadmon of Samos. Samos is a Greek island in the Aegean Sea.

Whenever I think of Aesop, I think of fables. Aesop was, to me, the Father of Fables. Webster's dictionary defines a fable as "a fictitious story meant to teach a moral lesson: the characters are usually animals." Aesop's fables are vignette's suitable for young children. (This is the first time I have used the word "vignette." I had heard it bandied about in several writing classes but never really understood its meaning. Webster's dictionary defines vignette as "a short literary composition characterized by compactness, subtlety, and delicacy." Who would deny that Aesop's Fables are vignettes?) I have read dozens of his fables, both in English and in German. A book of Aesop's fables makes a great gift to young children, to introduce them to reading, and the world of ideas, and to include as one of the first volumes in their personal library.

I believe that Aesop may have been of African origin. Vignettes using animals endowed with speech to teach moral lessons is a common theme in many African cultures. Africa has a multitude of rich cultures and languages. The ancient Greeks called anyone from Africa an "Ethiop." Perhaps Aesop is a corruption of the word

"Ethiop."

Aesop's fables have been translated into most of the major languages of the world. They have been enjoyed by people all over the world for over two thousand six hundred years. Millions of people the world over have benefited from their moral lessons. Surely Aesop must rank as one of the greatest teachers of all time.

Shakespeare didn't get many things wrong but he may have erred when he had Mark Antony, in his funeral oration for Julius Caesar say "The evil men do lives after them. The good is oft interred with their bones." Aesop died about 560 BC. No one knows exactly when. Millions of people, all over the world, revere the memory of Aesop, the slave. Who remembers his master Iadmon of Samos?

I have seven or eight books of Aesop's fables in my home library. I have endeavored to use them to learn how to write poetry. First, I rewrite the fable in my own words and extract the moral, again in my own words, in prose. Then I tell the fable as poetry in rhymed couplets of ten syllables per line. It is fun.

— Carl J. Hasper

# 1

## A MAN WITH TWO WIVES

A man, in olden times when it was legal, had two wives. One of the wives was older than the man and the other was younger. They both loved him very much and all three of them were pleased when the two wives groomed the man.

The man was middle aged and beginning to get some grey hairs. The younger wife thought he looked a bit too old for her, so when she brushed his hair, she secretly plucked grey hairs every time she had a chance.

The older wife thought he looked too young for her, so when she combed his hair, she secretly plucked dark hairs every time she had a chance.

If you have been paying attention to this tale told by Aesop you have probably guessed that it wasn't long until the man was totally bald, and his pate as smooth as a melon.

MORAL: Polygamy is not good for your hair.

## TWO WIVES AND THEIR HUSBAND

Long ago Polygamy was legal
Whether or not you were poor or Regal.
In that time there was a Man with two Wives
And all of them lived very happy lives.

The trio was happy when he was groomed.
This poem will relate how his hair was doomed.
The stress of two Wives chattering all day
Was such that the Man began to get grey

He looked too old for her, with the grey hair,
Thought his young Wife, who was pretty and fair,
So when she brushed his hair, she plucked the grey,
Whenever she groomed his hair every day.

He looked too young for her, with the dark hair,
Thought his old Wife, who was grey, and not fair,
And so when she combed his hair she would pluck
His dark hairs, thinking that would bring her luck.

If you have paid attention to this tale
Told long ago by Aesop to regale
Then by now you must have guessed the Man's fate.
He's as bald as a melon, on his pate.

— Carl J. Hasper

## 2

## A TALE OF A TAIL

A Fox was caught in a Trap. The only way he could extricate himself was by leaving his Tail in the Trap. Without his Tail he felt naked and ashamed. A Fox's Tail is a useful appendage. When fleeing, it acts as a counterweight so he can change direction rapidly when pursued by Dogs, and thereby avoid being caught. On a cold Night he can curl up with it and it acts as a blanket to help him to keep warm.

In the town meeting hall in Foxtown, he tried to make light of his misfortune and tried to convince the other Foxes to remove their own Tails. He said, "I never realized how happy I'd be without a Tail. I no longer need that ugly, useless Tail dragging after me. I should have done this long ago. Why don't the rest of you join me and remove your Tails also?"

A sly old Fox in the back of the room said, "You are a good orator and have made a cogent case for us Foxes to remove our Tails. If I had lost mine in an accident as you did, I might agree, but I like my tail as it is, and intend to keep it."

MORAL: Be wary of Town Hall proposals.

## THE TALE IN THE TAIL

A Fox had an unfortunate mishap
And found himself caught inside a Trap
And the only way he could get free
Was to leave his Tail, entrapped, by a Tree.

Loss of a Tail, you may think, no big deal
But to a Fox, the loss is very real.
He felt naked and ashamed without his Tail
And it caused him a great deal of travail.

He was the only Fox without a Tail
And this was not just a minor detail
So the other Foxes, he did regale
With reasons why each should remove his Tail.

In Foxtown they had a Town Meeting Hall.
'Twas a place to meet, with a voice for all.
Fox had an audience he could regale
And he began by berating his Tail.

"I wish I had lost my Tail long ago.
I'm glad it's gone. It was only for show.
No longer must I drag that ugly Tail.
With a sigh of relief, I can inhale."

"Tails are useless and we do not need them
So just take them off. It is not a Sin.
Follow my example. Remove your Tail.
Why drag it along over Hill and Dale?"

An old Fox spoke from the back of the Room
His voice resonant as in a Tomb.
"I'll grant that you are a good Orator
That no longer has a Tail anymore."

"I'm sorry for you, that you lost your Tail.
It no longer follows you on the Trail.
I love my Tail, 'tho it's Fluffy and frail,
As it follows me over Hill and Dale."

"As for me, I'll ignore your suggestion.
With my Tail, my Children, have lots of fun."

— Carl J. Hasper

## 3

## HERCULES AND THE WAGONER

A Farmer was driving his heavily laden Wagon carelessly on a muddy Road, heedless of the hazards. The Wheels got stuck in some wet Clay and no matter how forcefully he urged the Horses, they were unable to free it. Without assessing the situation further to see how he, himself, might assist the Horses to extricate the Wagon, he called upon Hercules to assist him. Hercules soon appeared and directed the man to grab the back Spoke of the Wheel and lift up and at the same time direct the Horses to pull. He did so and the Wagon immediately moved forward and the Wheel was freed from the Clay. Hercules scolded the man for 1.) carelessly driving the Wagon into the wet Clay, and 2.) not, himself, figuring out how to free it. He reminded him that the Gods are busy and only help those who help themselves.

MORAL: 1. Try not to drive yourself into a Quagmire.

MORAL: 2. If you find yourself in a Quagmire, at least try to extricate yourself before calling upon others for help.

## THE WAGONER AND HERCULES

A man drove a Wagon on a wet Road.
The Wagon was laden with a heavy Load.
Heedless of the hazards of the wet Road
He drove through puddles with the heavy Load.

A Wheel sank deep into Clay that was wet.
The Wagon stopped as if the Brake were set.
He urged the Horses, but they could not go
'Cause the Clay was as thick as baking Dough.

He urged the Horses, but they could not move.
A Wheel was stuck in a deep Groove.
He knew not what to do, nor did he try.
In desperation, he reached to the Sky.

He called on Hercules to come help him.
Hercules soon appeared, his visage dim.
The Clouds disappeared, and the Sky turned blue
As Hercules told the man what to do.

"Just lift the back Spoke of the Wagon Wheel
Put your back into it and show some zeal
Now lift the Spoke, and urge the Horses on."
As if it were pulled by a Mastodon

The Wagon surged forward, and it was free.
"In the future, you must not bother me.
Gods are too busy to help everyone.
Try it yourself, and you can get it done."

— Carl J. Hasper

# 4

## MOTHER CRAB AND BABY CRAB

A Mother Crab chided her child for not walking straight. The Baby Crab replied, “Mom, show me the way and I’ll follow you.”

MORAL: Actions speak louder than words.

## BABY CRAB AND MOTHER CRAB

Mother Crab said, "You must walk straight, my dear."
To her baby, following in the rear.
"I will follow you, Mom. You lead the way."
Said Baby, "And I will not go astray."

If you want your children to do what's right
Set an example, and show them the light.

— Carl J. Hasper

## 5

## THE AMOROUS LION AND THE WOODCUTTER AND HIS DAUGHTER

A Lion in the Forest, in love with a Woodcutter's Daughter, asked for her Hand in Marriage. When the Woodcutter, shocked by the thought of such an incongruous alliance with his beautiful Daughter declined, the Lion roared his disappointment and frightened the Woodcutter. The Woodcutter, although frightened, kept his wits, and said to the Lion "Great King, I was flattered by your proposal but fear for my frail Daughter. Your powerful Teeth and Claws would certainly bruise her delicate person. If you will agree to have your powerful Teeth pulled and Claws removed, I will gladly agree to your proposal."

When the Lion agreed and all was done, the Woodcutter took his Axe and drove the toothless and clawless Lion from his Cottage.

MORAL: Disarmament is a dangerous Strategy.

## THE WOODCUTTER, HIS DAUGHTER, AND THE AMOROUS LION

This Story was told to me by a Bird
And it may sound to you just a wee bit absurd.
A big Lion, not timid like a Mouse
Walked right on in to a Woodcutter's House.

The Woodcutter stepped back. "Fee Fie Foe Fum.
Where ever did this big Kitty come from?"
"I'm in Love, and I beg, I don't demand.
I love your Daughter. May I have her Hand?"

"Mister Lion, you are a Noble Beast.
It would be nice to have a Wedding Feast.
You are Gracious and Polite and not Curt
But I'm afraid my Daughter might get hurt."

"You are so big and my Daughter so frail.
Why, my Daughter is as thin as a Rail.
For all of these reasons I must say no.
And I will tell you now that you must go."

When the Great Big Lion let out a Roar,
The Woodsman almost fainted on the Floor.
But despite his Fear the Woodsman was brave.
He thought of how, his Daughter, he could save.

To remove all of his Teeth, Lion agreed
And when they were all gone, he did not bleed.
To remove all of his Claws, he agreed
And when they were all gone, he did not bleed.

"Now that I have done all that you demand
May we be married? May I have her Hand?"
"No Mister Lion. This may sound unkind.
You'd better get out. I've changed my Mind."

And he swung his Axe, and the Lion fled
Toothless and Clawless. They never were Wed.

— Carl J. Hasper

6

## THE ANT AND THE DOVE

A tiny Ant, walking at the edge of a small Pool of Water, accidentally fell into the Water. The Ant struggled to reach the Shore, all to no avail, and was about to perish. A Dove, perched on a Limb of a nearby Tree, observed the predicament of the Ant, took pity on him, and dropped a Leaf into the Water adjacent to him. The Ant was able to scramble onto the Leaf. The Leaf was a Life Raft for the Ant. A gentle Breeze blew the Leaf, and the Ant, to the Shore. The grateful Ant hurried away.

Some time later, the Ant observed, as a Man stealthily maneuvered to deploy a Net used to catch Birds. He was about to ensnare the unsuspecting Dove when the Ant bit him on the Ankle. Startled, the Man dropped the Net and the Dove escaped.

MORAL: One good turn deserves another.

## THE DOVE AND THE ANT

A long, long time ago in Days of yore
A Tiny Ant hurried along a Shore.
There was no Ocean Wave nor Tidal Bore.
There was nothing to cause an Ocean's Roar.

To an Ant, a Puddle is an Ocean
And the Ant was on a Beach excursion.
He suddenly tumbled into the Bay
Into the Water, much to his dismay.

As he struggled in the Water to survive
Flailing all about, and barely alive
A Dove, on a Limb, observed his distress,
Took pity on the Ant, who was helpless

Placed a Leaf in the Water alongside
And the Ant clambered aboard for a ride.
Soon a Gentle Breeze wafted them ashore.
The small Ant was grateful, forevermore.

A few Days later in the Early Morn
The Ant was walking in a Field of Corn.
The Ant observed a Man, suspiciously
As he crept, with a Net, under a Tree.

A Man with a Net, sneaked up on the Dove
His Friend, the Dove, he remembered with Love.
Slowly he lifted the Net, high above
About to toss the Net over the Dove.

The Man was ready to pounce with the Net.
His Friend, the Dove, the Ant did not forget.
He bit the Man on the Ankle and ran
As the Net dropped, on the Head, of the Man

And the Dove escaped, and she flew away,
Thrilled to be alive for another Day.

— Carl J. Hasper

# 7

## THE ARCHER AND THE LION

An Archer came into a field in search of game. As soon as they were aware of his presence, the beasts all became terrified and fled. All, that is, but one. The Lion stood his ground and challenged the Archer to combat. "Hey! Mr. Lion! My messenger has a message for you!" said the Archer as he launched his dart. It struck the Lion, who, wounded and in extreme pain, fled the scene. As he passed a Fox, the Fox tried to persuade him to return to the fray. "No way!" said the Lion. "If a mere messenger can inflict such pain, I don't want to fight with his master!"

A Lion has powerful weapons, sharp teeth, powerful jaws and sharp claws and is fast. An Archer's arrow has a long range and is faster.

MORAL: Military Science 101. A fast, long range weapon trumps a slower one of short range, every time.

## THE LION AND THE ARCHER

Into the wilderness, an Archer came.
The Archer strode forward, looking for game.
The animals were wild, they were not tame.
When they saw him, they fled, even the lame.

Only the king, the Lion, stood his ground.
He boldly walked forward, to a small mound.
The confident Archer, too, stood his ground.
He turned toward the Lion, and voiced this sound

"Mr. Lion, I've a message for you."
Like lightning, from his bow, an arrow flew.
The dart struck the Lion. In pain he fled.
A trickle of blood, from the wound, he bled.

A sad thing to see, a terrible sight
To see their king run, to see their king's fright,
Passing all others, much to their dismay.
Only the Fox thought of something to say.

The Fox told him to return to the fray.
Replied the Lion to the Fox "No way!
I saw the Man's bow and heard its string twang.
It wasn't long until I felt the pang,

The pain from his messenger, a mere dart.
For a conflict with him, I have no heart."

— Carl J. Hasper

## 8

## THE ASS'S SHADOW

Long ago in Athens on a hot Summer Day a Traveler hired an Ass and its Driver to transport himself and his baggage from Athens to Megara. Already, in those days, in the sixth Century before Christ, the Forests of Ancient Greece had been removed, first to build Warships, oared Galleys built of Wood, and then to make Charcoal to create Fires hot enough to smelt Metals needed to make Armor to protect Soldiers, and to make the Weapons needed to kill their Enemies. Without the Roots of the Trees to hold the Soil in place, the Rains washed it away, and the underlying Rock, the Bones of Mother Earth, protruded into the Sky. With the topsoil gone, farms could no longer raise the Crops of Grain needed to make Bread. Cash Crops of Olives and Grapes, which grew in the poor Soil were raised instead, to make Oil and Wine that were traded with Farms around the Black Sea, in exchange for Grains for Bread.

The Forest cover no longer provided Shade and by mid-afternoon, the intense Heat induced the traveler to call a halt. Global Warming had begun. He wanted to lie down in the Shadow of the Ass, to cool off before continuing his Journey. The Driver said, "You hired the Donkey, not his Shadow, and if we're going to stop, I'll rest in his Shadow." An altercation ensued, and while they were arguing about who had the right to use the Ass's Shadow, the Ass, seizing the opportunity, fled to freedom, and brought the Shadow with him.

MORAL: If you quarrel about the Shadow of a thing, you may lose the Essence of the thing itself.

## THE SHADOW OF THE ASS

In Ancient Athens on a Summer Day
A Traveler asked, "How much must I pay
To hire an Ass, and a Driver, too?
In Megara, I have a rendezvous."

He found a good Ass, and a Driver, too.
They all hurried off for the rendezvous.
The Road was only a rut in the Grass.
The Traveler was hot as he rode the Ass.

Global Warming had already begun.
It was hot, without Trees, under the Sun.
To make Ships, for War, they cut down the trees
To fabricate Ships to capture the Breeze.

Long rows of Oars for Biremes and Triremes
The long rows of Oars were pulled by Marines.
Under Water, at the Prow, was a Ram.
It was clad in Bronze and designed to jam

Into an Enemy Ship and sink it
When the Sides of the Ship splintered and split.
Bronze, an Alloy of Copper and Tin
Made Helmets and Breast Plates to protect men

Spear Points and Arrow Heads to penetrate
Deep into the Flesh, under a Breast Plate.
They needed Bronze, to protect, and to Kill,
To protect, as they sought, Victory's Thrill.

Copper and Tin were expensive and rare.
Iron Ore could be found almost everywhere.
Smelting of Iron needed a hotter Fire
Charcoal and Bellows to blow on the Fire.

They had not yet discovered the Rock, Coal.
Instead, they had to make, from Wood, Charcoal
And they made Fires, using Charcoal, to burn,
To get Fires hot enough to melt the Iron.

So they cut down Trees to make Ships, for War
And more Trees in order to smelt the Ore.
Without Roots of Trees, topsoil washed away.
You can see outcrops of Rocks yet today.

And the bare Rocks protrude into the Sky
Like the Bleached Bone of Mother Earth's Thigh.
Grassy Plains were hot without the Forest
And the traveler said "I've got to rest."

"Stop. I'll lie in the Shadow of the Ass."
The Driver said, " You've got a lot of Brass!
You rented the Donkey, not his Shadow.
For the use of his Shade, you must pay more Dough!"

As they argued, hot under the Collar,
Who had the right, Driver or Traveler,
Using every Word in the Lexicon
The Ass wandered away, and soon was gone.

They lost the Donkey, and his Shadow, too
Under a Sky of Cerulean Blue.

— Carl J. Hasper

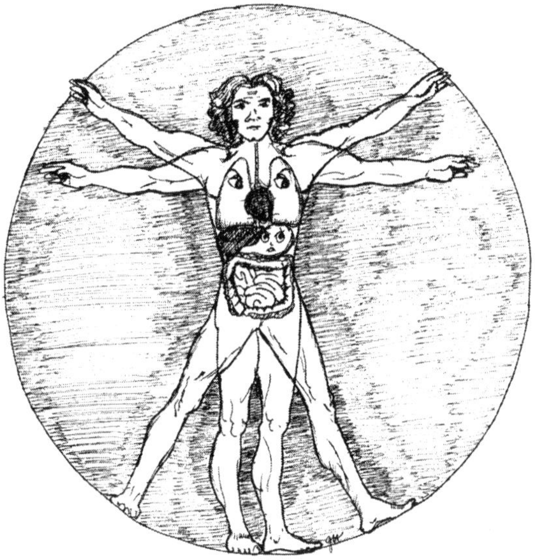

# 9

## THE BELLY VERSUS THE OTHER BODY PARTS

There was a time, ages ago, when the various body parts had strong wills of their own and did not always work together for the betterment of the whole. The Belly, in particular, was denounced by the other body parts for doing nothing, while the other body parts had to support it. The Hands had to deliver Food to the Mouth, the Teeth had to chew it and the Esophagus had to deliver the Bolus to the Stomach, and the Feet and Legs had to carry the big, lazy, good-for-nothing Belly along wherever the Mind told them to go. This had to stop, so all the other body parts agreed to go on strike. They would no longer support the Belly. The Hands would no longer deliver Food to the Mouth. The Teeth would no longer chew the Food, and the Esophagus would no longer deliver the Bolus to the Stomach.

Alas, not just the Belly, but all the other body parts began to atrophy and waste away. The body parts conferred about this sorry result. They decided that perhaps the Belly was performing some necessary function they were unaware of, and needed, for their own welfare. They called off their strike, and all the body parts became healthy again, including the Belly.

MORAL: Parts must work together for the betterment of the whole.

## THE OTHER BODY PARTS VERSUS THE BELLY

Ages ago the Parts of the Body
Were different than they are today, and free.
They talked together and complained a lot.
They weren't just a big Organic Robot.

The Belly, they said, was good for nothing
And, they said, they had to do everything.
The Hand, to the Mouth, had to bring the Food.
The Tongue moved the Food, while the Teeth chewed.

Food, swallowed into the Esophagus,
Esophagus delivered the Bolus.
The Bolus delivered to the Stomach
Where it was squeezed and churned into a Muck.

The Mind told the Legs where to place the Feet
When the Belly was moved along the Street.
The big, lazy, good-for nothing Belly
That moved about like a Bowl of Jelly.

From this abject Slavery they must be freed.
To go on Strike, they all agreed.
Hand, to the Mouth, would no longer bring Food.
Tongue did not move, and Teeth no longer chewed.

Nothing for the Esophagus to do
Because the Teeth did not have Food to chew.
But, alas, everything did not go well
Something that this Poem will now need to tell.

Not only the Belly began to ail.
The other Body Parts began to fail.
They began to get weak and lose their strength
So they discussed their problem at great length.

The Body Parts conferred about this
In order find out what was amiss.
The Body was weak and ready to fall.
The Belly might be needed after all.

They decided to call off their Strike
A decision they did not all like.
They agreed to serve the Belly again.
Their Health improved like a Crop after Rain.

They agreed to serve the Belly again.
Every one was happy. No one had Pain.

— Carl J. Hasper

## 10

## THE CANDLE WITH AN EGO

Long ago, in the Dining Hall of a King's Castle, on the Table, was a large, beautiful Beeswax Candle. Every evening, just before the King's Guests arrived for Dinner, the Candle's Wick was ignited and the Candle glowed with a bright, mellow, beautiful flame. It exuded the Fragrance of the Nectar the Bees had collected from beautiful, aromatic Flowers and brought to the Hive that was the source of the Beeswax the Candle was made of.

The important, erudite Guests often complimented the King for having the most beautiful, and brightest Candlelight anywhere. The Candle, hearing the comments of praise, made the egotistical comment "Indeed. My Light is more brilliant than that of the Sun, the Moon, and all of the Stars together." The Wind outside roared, and a puff of Air from a Draft extinguished the Candle. As he re-ignited the Candle, the Servant cautioned "Beware. This is a warning from the Gods. The Gods are angry when mere Mortals compare their abilities with those of the Gods. A puff of Air extinguished your Light. The Lights of Heaven are never extinguished."

MORAL: Whatever you do can never compare with the works of the Gods. Do not anger them by boasting.

## THE EGO OF THE CANDLE

There was a Candle made of Wax from Bees,
Collectors of Pollen, that makes us sneeze.
It was a large Candle on a Table.
I'll tell you about it in this Fable.

'Twas on the Dining Table of a King
And the Invited Guests were gathering.
A King's Servant went to the Fireplace.
The Servant walked slowly. He did not race.

Into the Flames, he put the end of a Stick
And he brought a Flame to the Candle's Wick.
When the Flames melted the Wax in the Wick
The Wax evaporated. It was quick.

From the hot, melted Wax, came a Vapor.
It's burning Vapor that lights a Taper.
The candle ignited. Its Glow was Bright
And it burned away the Darkness of Night.

The Candle glowed with a Bright Mellow Flame.
Its magnificent Beauty gave it Fame.
It exuded a most pleasant Fragrance
That supplemented its Magnificence.

The Candles Brightness lit up the Kings Hall,
Reflected off Gold Paintings on the Wall.
Perhaps it was the Wonderful Fragrance
That put all of the Guests into a Trance.

Important, Erudite Guests were entranced.
An Acrobatic Troupe did Flips and Danced.
The Candle at the center of the Room
Emitted a Light that chased away the Gloom.

"It's more Golden than the Golden Sun!"
"More Silvery than the Silvery Moon!"
"The Stars above, with Envy, must be Green!"
"The most Beautiful Light I've ever seen!"

"Sire, I've never seen a Candle so Bright!"
"The Gods above must be pleased with its Light!"
It's because Aesop lived in Pagan times
That Poets use Pagan Gods in their Rhymes.

It's because Candles are not truly Dead
The Compliments went to the Candle's Head.
"For Light, I am one of its Avatars,
Brighter than the Sun, the Moon, and the Stars."

The Candle was Dumb, but it was not Dead.
It was a Blasphemous Thing that it said.
Some say it was because the Candle sinned
That a Storm arose with a Howling Wind.

The Guests could hear it with their Ears
And in many of them it aroused Fears.
When a Gust of Wind blew the Candle out
Everyone knew, and no one had a doubt.

Its light extinguished by a Puff of Air
A warning to the Candle to Beware.
The Kings Servant went to the Fireplace.
The Servant walked slowly. He did not race.

Into the Flames, he put the end of a Stick
And he brought a Flame to the Candles Wick.
As he lit the Wick, he gave it caution.
"Don't ever compare your Light to the Sun!"

"This was a warning from the Gods. Beware!
Your Light extinguished by a Puff of Air.
Their Lights are never extinguished up there.
To Heavenly Lights, yours does not compare!"

— Carl J. Hasper

## 11

## THE CRAFTY LION AND THE WARY FOX

A Lion was getting old. He was missing some Teeth. Arthritis was taking its toll and slowing him down. He was having more and more difficulty in capturing prey, and losing weight. The Crafty Lion decided upon a ruse. He announced that he was dying and would retire to his Den, a Cave in the Hillside, and would welcome visitors who came to pay their last respects. After all, he was the King of the Forest.

Some Animals were taken in by the ruse. One at a time, they came to see him, bringing gifts. One day a Silly Goose came, the next day a Timid Sheep, and a few days later a Dumb Ass. Each was graciously welcomed into the Den by the Lion. He made them feel at ease and, at the opportune moment, the Lion pounced upon the gullible victim and devoured her (or him).

A Sly Fox cautiously approached the entrance to the Lion's Den and called out "Hello. Is anyone home?" The Lion replied "My old friend, Mister Fox. I've always admired you, especially your magnificent Tail. Unfortunately, I've had to admire it from afar. I'm on my deathbed now. Come inside so I can admire it up close, before I die." The Wary Fox replied "Thank you for inviting me into your Den, Your Majesty, but I must decline for now. I can see by all the footprints entering your Den and none coming out, you must have many guests right now. I'll stop by later." The Fox went on his way.

MORAL: Be Wary and Beware.

## THE WARY FOX AND THE CRAFTY LION

The King of the Forest was growing old.
He was slowing down, no longer so bold.
He had a broken Tooth, arthritic pain,
Missing Claws, a lame Foot and Mangy Mane.

But in spite of all his arthritic pain
The Crafty Lion yet had his Brain.
A Martial Expert knows how to defend
By yielding like a Willow in the Wind.

The Lion would use illness, to pretend,
Instead, and so he did not need the Wind.
He let it be known that he was dying
And some did not suspect he was lying.

A Silly Goose came to pay him respect.
She was gullible and not circumspect
And the Lion's friendly voice disarmed her.
"I'm pleased to see you." She was his dinner.

A Timid little Sheep enticed inside.
Was it Murder or was it Suicide?
A Stupid Ass also came to visit.
Invited inside, he did not exit.

A Fox, always suspicious and Wary,
Useful traits which are hereditary,
Reconnoitered outside the Lion's Den
Before deciding if he should go in.

There were many footprints outside the Den.
None of them came out. They only went in.
"Hello there, inside of the Lion's Den.
I've come to visit. Is anyone in?"

The Lion recognized the Fox's voice
And he was hungry and he did rejoice.
"It's my old Friend, Mister Fox." he replied.
The Wary Fox knew that the Lion lied.

"I admire your Magnificent Tail
But always saw it from across the Dale.
I have always viewed it from far away.
How much does your Magnificent Tail weigh?"

"Come inside so I can see it close up.
I have some red Wine. Come, and share a Cup."
"Thanks for inviting me into your Den,
Your Majesty." He said with a Sly Grin.

"By the Footprints I see that all go in
And none come out, you have a crowded Den.
Some other time. For now I must decline."
And he sped away, into the Sunshine.

— Carl J. Hasper

## 12

## THE CROW'S EPIPHANY

A Crow was dying of thirst, when he spied a glass bottle with some water in it. Happily he approached the bottle, but his happiness turned to dismay, when he discovered that the bottle neck was too narrow for him to reach the water inside. He thought to himself, "If I turn it over, or break it, the water will soak into the desert sand." Suddenly an idea occurred to him. He selected some small pebbles that he dropped into the bottle. The pebbles sank to the bottom, the water level rose, he got his drink, and, contented, went on his way.

MORAL: Necessity gives birth to invention.

## THE EPIPHANY OF THE CROW

Weak with thirst was a Crow in the desert.
He stumbled around in the sand and dirt.
His throat was parched, and his long tongue hung out.
"But why me, oh Lord?" he said in a pout.

The Crow was dying when what did he see?
A bottle with water. He smiled with glee.
To the bottle he hurried, then came near
To the light brown bottle, that once held beer.

But when he got close, his eye dropped a tear.
He was again gripped by a gnawing fear.
The bottle's opening was far too small
And he could not reach the water at all.

He thought to himself, "I can not break it.
It will drain into the sand. Every bit.
Let me think now. I could tip it over,
And give a drink to that four leaf clover."

But now our crow had an Epiphany.
He had an idea, worth more than money.
Over to the bed of a dried up creek
He went, and picked up pebbles with his beak,

Took them to the bottle and let them drop
Into the water with a little pop.
You've got to admit that this Crow was wise.
The dropped in pebbles made the water rise.

He was so thirsty he could hardly think.
At last he was able to get a drink.
"But why me, Lord?" he had been heard to say.
God thanked him for remembering to pray.

His face lit up and he let out a cheer.
It was not water, but instead was beer!

— Carl J. Hasper

## 13

## THE DOG AND THE REFLECTION

A greedy Dog stole a piece of meat from a butcher shop. He fled, with the meat in his mouth, seeking a safe place to dine. It was a quiet day with no wind. As he traversed a small brook, he looked into the water and saw another dog with a similar piece of meat, looking up at him. Greedily, he snapped at the other dog's meat, in an attempt to seize it, but dropped his own piece of meat in the attempt. It splashed into the water and sank. The resulting ripples on the water erased the image of the dog in the water with a piece of meat looking up at him. Puzzled by the unexpected turn of events, the Dog turned away, with an empty stomach, again in search of a meal.

MORAL: Be satisfied with what you have. Don't try to take from others what you don't need for yourself, or you may lose what you have.

## THE REFLECTION AND THE DOG

A Dog was hungry and in search of food.
He was not in a very pleasant mood.
He trotted along the streets of a town
Looking here, and looking there, with a frown.

He was led by his nose along a street,
Perhaps by the aroma of fresh meat
Displayed at the front of a butcher's shop.
His mouth watered with a saliva drop.

With skillful patience he waited to see
A favorable opportunity
To seize a portion of the butcher's meat
For his breakfast meal. It would be a treat.

For the meat, he had no money to pay,
And waited 'til the butcher looked away.
When the butcher went back into the store
He seized some meat, and down the street, he tore.

At a safe distance, he slackened his pace.
There was no need to continue to race.
There was no wind, and the weather was fine.
He went on in search of a place to dine.

He traversed a small bridge over a rill,
Looked into the water and got a thrill.
There was another dog, also with meat.
He snapped at it to get another treat.

But alas! His meat in the water dropped.
Into the water it dropped with a plop!
Sank to the bottom. Was eaten by eels.
The Dog's greed had cost him both of his meals.

— Carl J. Hasper

## 14

### THE DOG IN THE MANGER

A Manger in a Barn contained Hay for the Horses. Each Day the Farmer came and filled it with Fresh Hay. One Day a Mangy Dog made his Bed in the Hay in the Manger and when the Horses came to eat, he growled and snarled to keep them away. "What a miserable Creature," said one Horse to another "He cannot eat the Hay himself,` but yet will not allow us to eat." When the Farmer came to put Fresh Hay in the Manger and saw the Dog, he drove it away with a Pitchfork.

MORAL: Use a thing in the manner in which it was designed to be used and do not deny it to others.

## THE DOG IN THE MANGER

A Manger in a Barn contained some Hay
Used to feed the Horses. It was their Pay
For all of the Work they did every Day.
Each Day the Farmer filled it with Fresh Hay.

One Fine Day a Mangy Dog made his Bed
In the Manger from which the Horses fed
And when the Horses came to eat their Hay
He growled and snarled and kept them at Bay.

A Horse said, "He's a miserable Cur
And reclines on our Hay with Mangy Fur.
Even though he cannot use the Hay to eat
He will not allow us to eat our Treat."

The Farmer came with Fresh Hay for the Manger
And saw the Dog in the Hay, a Stranger.
"I'll teach you a lesson, you Dirty Lout
And with this Pitchfork, I will drive you out."

— Carl J. Hasper

## 15

## THE EAGLE AND THE ARROW

A Hunter with a Bow took aim at an Eagle as it soared overhead. The Arrow sped upwards and struck the Eagle in the Breast. In the agony of death as it plunged downward, the Eagle saw that the Arrow had been fletched with its own Feathers and said, "How much more painful it is to know that my own Feathers were used to make the Weapon of my destruction!"

MORAL: Death is bad enough but even worse when the Victim helped to make the weapon of his own destruction.

## THE ARROW AND THE EAGLE

A Hunter with a Bow looked to the Sky.
Lo and Behold! An Eagle he did spy.
The Man stood on the Shore of a River
Selected an Arrow from his Quiver

And fitting the Arrow to the Bowstring
He pulled and aimed and let fly with a ping.
The Arrow sped upwards, on its course true
And struck and killed the Eagle as it flew.

As he plummeted down in agony
His Feathers, in the Arrow, he could see.
"It is much more painful," the Eagle said
"My own Feathers were used to make me dead."

"My own Feathers used to guide the Arrow.
They guided it true, to my own sorrow.
My own Feathers used to fletch the Arrow
Causes double Pain and double Sorrow!"

— Carl J. Hasper

Comment: On September 11, 2001, there were four Arrows of our own making that were guided into the Breasts of our Innocents.

## 16

## THE EAGLE AND THE ARROW (Version 2) *

As an Eagle soared in the Sky, an Archer took aim and launched a Dart which struck the Eagle in the Breast and penetrated his Heart. As the Eagle tumbled toward the Earth below, he observed the Arrow that struck the fatal blow and noticed that it was fletched with his own Feathers, and said "It's doubly painful to realize I helped supply the Weapon that killed me."

MORAL: We may suffer consequences even if we unknowingly contribute to the production of lethal weapons.

## THE ARROW AND THE EAGLE (Version 2)

An Eagle soared gracefully in the Sky
With nary an inkling that he might die.
On the Ground below an Archer took aim
And fired a Dart that could Kill or Maim.

Not a single Cloud 'cause the Day was Fair
As the Arrow cut its way through the Air.
Deep into the Eagle's Chest sped the Dart.
It's point came to rest in the Eagles Heart.

As the Eagle tumbled down from the Sky
He glimpsed the Arrows Feathers with his Eye.
His own Feathers fletched the end of the Dart
And helped direct it into his own Heart.

"Alas, what doubly painful irony
That my own Feathers should help to kill me!"

— Carl J. Hasper

* The reason there is a version 2 is that the author had forgotten he had already written it a few years earlier, and only realized it when he attempted to save it as a file and found there was already a file by that name. Notice how different they are, and yet how alike.

## 17

## THE FOX AND THE CROW

A young couple picnicked by a country stream. They had brought a Loaf of Bread, a Flask of Wine, themselves, and a large piece of Cheese. Unbeknownst to them, while they were dining, a hungry Fox was watching from concealment for an opportunity to seize and make off with something to eat. The Fox, a Vixen, needed to bring food back to her Kits in their burrow on the hillside. It was a warm summer afternoon and when the couple decided to cool off in the inviting water of the Stream, leaving their food on a cloth they had spread on the ground, a Crow, who had also been watching, and waiting for an opportunity, swooped down, seized the piece of Cheese that remained on the cloth, and perched on a limb of a nearby Tree with the piece of Cheese in its mouth. The disappointed Fox did not give up but decided to use her wile (Foxes are known for being wily) to get the Cheese from the Crow. She trotted over to the Tree, looked up admiringly at the Crow, and said "What a beautiful Bird you are! Your Feathers are as iridescent as those of a Peacock, and Talons as powerful as those of an Eagle. You are magnificent! If only you could sing."

Each flattering remark was food for the ego of the vain Crow, and he believed every word to be true. He opened his mouth and said "Caw" whereupon the Cheese dropped from his mouth and fell. The Fox caught the Cheese in mid air and retired to her burrow to dine with her Kits.

MORAL 1: Flatterers can get what they need by flattery.

MORAL 2: Those who are flattered must beware lest they lose what they have.

## THE CROW AND THE FOX

"A Loaf of Bread, a Flask of Wine, and Thou
Beside me, singing Songs, is not enou.
It's Wilderness. We'll need more to be fed.
We will need some Cheese to go with the Bread."

In the Country, on the Bank of a Stream,
A young Couple in Love, as in a Dream.
Piece of Cheese on Bread, a sip of Wine
A Kiss on the Cheek in the bright Sunshine.

The Water in the Stream beckons to them
To shed their Clothes and come in for a swim.
Cool Water invites them in for a dip.
They decide to remove their Shoes and strip.

A Fox, out of sight, sitting on its Tush
Observed the events, from behind a Bush.
"Cause the Vixen needed Food for her Kits,
To get the Cheese, she had to use her Wits.

The Fox was ready to pounce on the Cheese
When from up above, floating on a Breeze,
A black Crow swoops down, and seizes the Prize,
Holds it in its Beak, and away it flies.

It perched on a Limb, the Cheese in its Beak.
The Fox trotted over to take a peek
And she said to the Crow "I admire you.
You're more beautiful than a Cockatoo."

"You are like an Eagle, so big and strong
And your Talons are powerful and long."
I know this assertion may sound absurd
But the Crow's ego believed every word.

"Your black Feathers gleam with iridescence.
If only you could sing with eloquence."
He wanted to prove he was like a King
And opened his mouth to prove he could sing.

"Caw" he said, and the Cheese fell down below.
It dropped from the mouth of the vain black Crow.
The Fox leaped into the Air from below
And grabbed the Cheese, and away she did go

Up the Hill to her Burrow in the Ground.
After a good meal, her Kits all slept sound.

— Carl J. Hasper

## 18

## THE FOX AND THE GRAPES

A hungry Fox found some delicious looking grapes hanging from a vine high on the limb of a dead tree. The fox jumped high into the air and tried to reach them. He tried many times, but he could not reach them. Finally he gave up and went away to search elsewhere for some food. As he left, he said to himself, "It's just as well. They're probably sour anyway."

MORAL: Losers sometimes disparage the prize they were unable to obtain.

## SOUR GRAPES

An old hungry Fox was looking for food,
Tired and angry, not in a good mood.
Wandering about in the forest green,
He was in a bad mood, and mighty mean.

He looked up above and what did he see?
Delicious grapes on the limb of a tree!
Our old Fox was mangy and flea bitten.
By the sight of the grapes he was smitten.

Then into the air in a giant leap,
He sprang high in the air and tried to reap
A harvest of the grapes for his repast.
Again and again, he tried and at last,

It was getting late, and try as he might,
He could not reach them in the waning light.
As he gave up at last, and walked away,
"Probably sour." He was heard to say.

— Carl J. Hasper

## 19

## THE FOX AND THE MAN

A Fox was being chased by a pack of Hounds followed by Hunters with guns on a Fox hunt. He had run for miles and they were hot on his trail. He was exhausted and would probably be caught soon when he happened upon a small cottage. A man, hearing the baying Hounds, came out to see what the matter was. The desperate Fox said to the Man "Please, Sir, may I hide in your outhouse? I'm afraid those Hounds will soon catch me, and the Hunters will kill me, just for sport." The Man, who was smoking a pipe, said, "Sure, be my guest."

When the Hunters arrived they asked the Man if he had seen the Fox. "No, I haven't seen any Fox" he said, but while he was speaking he used his pipe to point to the outhouse. The Hunters, not understanding his gestures, and believing him to be a bit daft, called the Hounds and continued on their way. As soon as they were gone, the Fox emerged from hiding and continued silently on his way. The Man saw him sneaking away and said "Aren't you even going to thank me for saving your life? How ungrateful you are!"

The Fox had heard what the Man had told the Hunters, but he had also observed his gestures with the pipe. He replied "I would have thanked you when I heard what you said, but then I saw you pointing your pipe at where I was, and you certainly don't deserve any thanks for that!"

MORAL: Saying one thing and doing another will not win any friends.

## THE MAN AND THE FOX

A little Fox was being chased by Hounds
And he ran very fast by leaps and bounds.
The Hounds were followed by Hunters on Horse.
The Hunters were equipped with guns, of course.

The little Fox, over the ground, did sail.
The Hounds and Hunters were hot on his trail.
The Fox was exhausted. He'd run for miles
Unable to elude them with his wiles.

From a house up ahead, a Man came out
To see what the ruckus was all about.
The Fox asked the Man if he could go hide
Behind the house, in the outhouse, outside.

"Please Sir, may I hide inside your outhouse?
I swear, I'll be as quiet as a mouse.
Those Hounds and Hunters are hot on my trail
And want to kill me and cut off my tail."

Then the Man, who was smoking a pipe, said
"I want to help you. Go right on ahead.
I don't want the Hunters to kill you dead."
Those were the words that the smoking Man said.

The Fox went into the outhouse and spied
Through a knothole, at the events outside.
One of the mounted Hunters was a Squire.
"Have you seen a small Fox?" he did inquire.

"No, I have not seen a Fox anywhere
And if I did I would tell you, I swear."
But the sneaky Man pointed with his pipe
Towards the outhouse that smelled overripe.

But none of the Hunters could comprehend
The message the Man was trying to send
So they called the Hounds and went on their way
And the Fox was safe for another day.

The Fox emerged slowly from the outhouse
And crept away as silent as a Mouse.
"You're not going to thank me? I saved your life.
And your tail was not cut off with a knife."

The Man hurled the words at the little Fox
Who had survived many of life's hard knocks.
The Fox had heard all that the Man had said
And he was thankful that he was not dead

But he had seen the gesture with the pipe
As he looked from the outhouse that was ripe.
"I would have thanked you. I heard what you said
But your pointing pipe could have made me dead."

— Carl J. Hasper

## *20*

## THE GNAT AND THE BULL

A Gnat buzzed around a Bulls Head for some time and finally landed on its Horn saying "Pardon me Mister Bull for sitting on your Horn. If my weight bothers you at all, I'll buzz off immediately." The Bull replied, "You're no bother at all. In fact I didn't even know you were there."

MORAL: The smaller the mind, the bigger the conceit.

## THE BULL AND THE GNAT

In a far away Land on a hot Day
A Gnat buzzed around in the Month of May.
The tiny Gnat buzzed around and around
The Head of a Bull with hardly a Sound.

Around and around, the Bull's Head, it flew.
There were no Clouds at all. The Sky was blue.
On the Bull's Horn, it decided to land
While the Bull was standing on some dry Sand.

"Oh. Mister Bull, you are looking forlorn.
Please pardon me for resting on your Horn.
If I'm too heavy, you need only say
And I'll immediately fly away."

The Bull looked up when he heard the Gnat's Sound
But could not see it when he looked around.
"That you were even there, I did not know
So there is no reason for you to go."

— Carl J. Hasper

## 21

## THE GOOSE THAT LAID THE GOLDEN EGGS

A Man had a Goose that laid a Golden Egg about once every Week. The Man was poor and wanted to buy many new things, and he was impatient. He said to himself, "If I kill the Goose I can take all the Eggs immediately." He killed the Goose, but alas, there were no Golden Eggs inside, and now he had no Eggs at all.

MORAL: Don't kill the Goose that lays the Golden Eggs.

## THE GOOSE THAT LAID THE GOLDEN EGGS

A Poor Man had a Goose that was a Freak.
It lay a Golden Egg once every Week.
He was impatient and said with a sigh
"There are many new things I want to buy."

"Golden Eggs are fine, but one thing I hate.
I want the Eggs now. I don't want to wait."
He was impatient and said with a sigh
"I will have to kill the Goose. It must die."

He killed the Goose. There was nothing inside.
"I am a greedy Fool." The Poor Man sighed.

— Carl J. Hasper

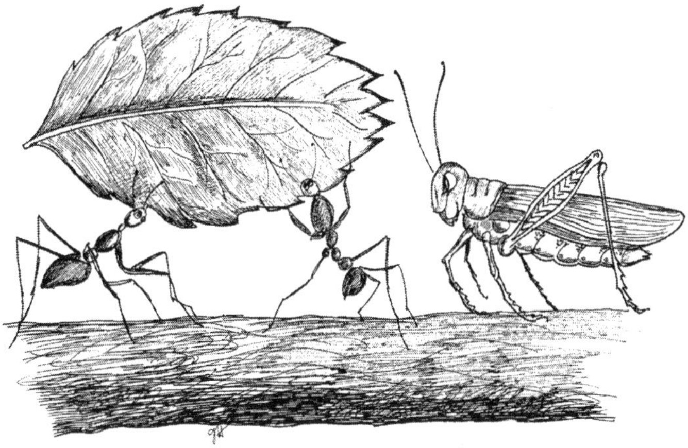

## 22

## THE GRASSHOPPER AND THE ANTS

The members of a colony of Ants worked hard all Summer and well into the Autumn gathering supplies to tide themselves over through the Winter. Ants are social insects and the Ant colony was a socialist endeavor. Some Ants dug tunnels and excavated underground rooms where the supplies could be stored. Other Ants brought the excavated debris above the ground and placed it so it would not roll back into the tunnels. Some Ants foraged for food and when they found it told the others where it was. They then cut the food into manageable size so it could be carried back and would fit into the tunnels to the supply rooms.

Times were good and they were amassing supplies they knew would be needed when Winter imposed harsh conditions such as frozen ground and snow cover and there was no longer any food to be had. They worked incessantly. The tunnels and storage rooms were their infrastructure. The supplies were the capital they could all share in the difficult times to come.

While the Ants were so busily occupied, a lone Grasshopper munched on grass and leaves when he was hungry, rested most of the time and poked fun at the industrious Ants. The ants were too busy to pay heed to him and continued their work.

Soon it was Autumn. The leaves dropped from the trees, grass turned brown and it became cold. The Grasshopper was hungry and shivering, and asked an Ant, who was bringing a last piece of food to the entrance of a supply tunnel, to share it with him. The Ant replied that the Grasshopper had not shared in the work and so could not share in the food, and continued on his way. Not long after, the Grasshopper died and the foraging Ants brought his remains into their supply room.

MORAL 1: Prepare yourself for bad times.

MORAL 2: You must share the pains to share the gains.

## THE ANTS AND THE GRASSHOPPER

Ants are social and all cooperate.
They are always on time and never late.
They're social insects that cooperate
To form a smooth running Socialist State.

When you look at these Ants who are so small
You would think they could not do much at all.
Certainly none of them is very tall
But to them, working is like playing ball.

The members of a colony of Ants
Composed of Cousins and Uncles and Aunts
Worked very hard. The work was shared by all.
They worked all Summer and into the Fall.

Some of the Ants dug tunnels underground
And others made rooms that were big and round
And some brought the Dirt up onto the ground
While other Ants spread the dirt all around.

Some Ants made storerooms that were big and round
To store food for the Winter underground.
Looking for food was the work of others.
A big Family, of Sisters and Brothers.

Some foraged for food, above ground, outside.
They were diligent, and searched far and wide.
If heavy and they could not carry it,
No problem. They cut it up, bit by bit.

If too large, into the tunnels to fit,
No problem. They cut it up, bit by bit.
Infrastructure for their economy,
The tunnels and storerooms, for all, were free.

Winter was coming and it would be harsh
No food anywhere and a frozen marsh.
And no longer any food to be had
The Ants knew the times coming would be bad.

Harvest time was an economic boom.
They stored food capital in the storeroom.
A big green Grasshopper just munched away
And when not eating, he engaged in play.

He poked fun at the Ants, and laughed at them
And said that their hard work was not for him.
Soon, leaves turned brown, and fell off of the Trees
And scattered on the ground, in a cold breeze.

And when the grass on the ground all turned brown
The shivering Grasshopper wore a frown.
A tiny Ant with a morsel of food
Put the Grasshopper in a better mood.

"My little Ant friend, would you care to share
That morsel of food? My cupboard is bare."
The Grasshopper smiled as he asked the Ant.
And the little Ant replied, "No, I can't."

"When times were good, we Ants worked very hard.
You strummed your guitar, and sang like a bard.
We Ants worked hard and you poked fun at us.
You are nothing but a lazy old Cuss."

And he entered the tunnel in the ground
As outside there was a foreboding sound
Of rustling leaves in the cold winter breeze,
Rustling Leaves that had fallen from the trees.

— Carl J. Hasper

## 23

# THE HARE AND THE TORTOISE

A big-mouthed Hare boasted of his athletic abilities, especially his ability to run fast, and poked fun at the lumbering gait of a Tortoise. The Tortoise, stung by the gratuitous insult, bet the Hare that he would beat him in a five-mile race. The Hare, cocksure of his superior ability to run fast, accepted the challenge. The Fox agreed to be the Judge.

A starting point was agreed upon, and the distance measured to the finish line. The Fox gave the starting signal and they were off. The Hare was off like a shot, leaving a trail of dust, and was soon out of sight. The Tortoise plodded along.

The Hare saw some tantalizing grass by the side

of the road and decided to stop and eat some of it. He was so far ahead he could not even see the Tortoise. After dining on the grass, the Hare decided he had plenty of time to take a nap in a sunlit patch of grass. When he awoke, he was startled to see the Tortoise near the finish line and hurried to catch up, but it was too late. The Tortoise had won.

MORAL: Slow but sure beats cocksure every time.

## THE TORTOISE AND THE HARE

A Hare was bragging how fast he could run
And at a slow Tortoise he poked some fun.
The Tortoise, in an effort to save face,
Challenged the Rabbit to a five mile Race.

In order to put the Hare in his place
The Tortoise challenged the Hare to a Race.
The Hare accepted the challenge with glee.
Mister Fox could judge, if he would agree.

Mister Fox agreed to judge the event
And he did not ask to be paid a Cent.
Fox measured five miles to the finish line.
He did not need a Clock to keep the time.

Fox gave the signal and they were both off.
The Tortoise, in the Hare's dust, had to cough.
In a cloud of dust, the Hare hummed a song.
The Tortoise steadily lumbered along.

Thinking the Tortoise was too slow to pass
The Hare stopped to eat some delicious grass.
Assuming the race was already won
The Hare decided to nap in the sun.

When the Hare awoke, it was almost Night.
He looked back. The Tortoise was not in sight.
The Dust had all settled and it was clear.
He decided he had nothing to fear.

But up ahead there was a roar, most loud,
A roar of approval from a big Crowd.
The Tortoise was the victor in the Race
Because he had maintained a steady pace.

— Carl J. Hasper

## 24
## THE LION AND FOUR BULLS

A hungry Lion often watched four Bulls in a grassy field. He knew that he could easily kill any one of them and have steak dinner for himself and his girl friend, the Lioness, for several days. But the four Bulls were good friends and always stayed together in the field, and the Lion knew that if he attacked any one of them, the others would come to its assistance and drive him away with their sharp horns.

Then the Lion had an idea, an epiphany. He started a whisper campaign about how one of the Bulls had made a disparaging remark about one of the others, and another of the Bulls had belittled the others, etc. The rumors sowed suspicion among the Bulls. Their friendship soured and soon each of the Bulls was grazing in a different part of the field.

It wasn't long before the Bulls were killed, one at a time, and the Lion and his girl friend were purring with contentment after their fine meals.

MORAL 1: Divide and Conquer.

MORAL 2: Beware of Gossip.

## THE FOUR BULLS AND A LION

One day a hungry Lion in a field
Attacked four Bulls but then he had to yield.
Mister Lion only wanted one Bull
More than enough to make his stomach full.

But the four courageous Bulls stood their ground
And their defensive strategy was sound.
Each time a Bull was attacked by the Lion
Another gored him and sent him cryin'

A big problem was faced by the Lion.
He was so hungry he was almost diein'
He had to get the Bulls to separate
So that he could determine their fate.

Then the Lion had an Epiphany.
The new idea he had was not zany.
He started a vicious whisper campaign.
Soon nasty remarks flew about like rain.

The whisper campaign that he had begun
Now grew its own legs and started to run.
One Bull, whose friend was like his own brother,
Was now said to belittle the other.

Another was said to make a wise crack
In a sneaky way, behind his friend's back.
The malicious rumors sowed suspicion
Amongst the Bulls who no longer had fun.

So each of the Bulls now went his own way.
They separated and went far away.
Mister Lion now had his own way.
Each of the lone Bulls was an easy prey.

— Carl J. Hasper

## *25*

## THE LION AND THE BEAR AND THE FOX

A Lion and a Bear pounced upon a Fawn at the same time. A vicious struggle for the prize ensued. They tore at each other with powerful Claws and Teeth and their Blood soaked into the Ground. The equal struggle continued until they both lay on the Ground, their Prey between them, unable to move. A Fox who had been watching, approached cautiously, seized the Carcass, and hurried away.

MORAL: Diplomacy is too often neglected.

## THE FOX AND THE LION AND THE BEAR

Two Predators with a great deal of Brawn,
A Lion and a Bear, pounced upon a Fawn.
The Fawn died quietly without a Sound.
Its Carcass lay between them on the Ground.

Both claimed the Prize. Neither of them ran
And a Struggle between them both began.
Powerful Claws, into tender Flesh tore.
Long sharp Teeth driveled Saliva and Gore.

Thunderous Roars spread Fear throughout the Land
And their Blood sprinkled across the Warm Sand.
As the gigantic Beasts struggled and bled
Small Animals like Birds and Squirrels fled.

The equal Struggle continued at length.
The Adversaries were equal in Strength.
Each one tried, his right to the Prize, to prove.
They fought until neither of them could move.

They fell exhausted, and lay on the Ground.
A small shy Fox approached without a Sound
And seized the Carcass and fled with a Bound.
The Lion and the Bear lay on the Ground.

— Carl J. Hasper

## 26
## THE LION AND THE MOUSE

On an African plain, at the edge of the forest, a mighty Lion, king of the forest, dozed in the shade of a baobab tree. A tiny Mouse, playing games with some friends, scampered across the face of the Lion. The Lion caught the Mouse in its mighty paw and held it in front of its huge face to see what it was that had disturbed its sleep. The terrified Mouse pleaded "Please, Mister Lion, I meant you no harm. Let me go, and perhaps some day I can return the favor." The mighty Lion was amused by the audacity of this tiny creature and said "Ho! Ho! Ho! A little runt like you help me? Run along, but don't disturb my sleep again." and released the tiny Mouse.

A few days later, the Mouse heard a mighty roar

in the forest and recognized it as that of the Lion who had let him go. Hunters had placed a net in the forest and the Lion was entangled in it, desperate to get out before the hunters came to take him away. His efforts to escape were futile and he was ready to accept his fate when the tiny Mouse came with several friends. They formed a line and each gnawed a piece of the cord of which the net was made. In a few moments a huge rent was made in the net. The astonished Lion thanked them and escaped.

MORAL: Don't underestimate the ability of a small friend.

## THE MOUSE AND THE LION

In the shade of a big baobab tree
Where African animals all run free
A big mighty Lion dozed in the shade
Dozed in the shade that the baobab made.

A tiny Mouse and his friends were playing
And did not notice where they were going.
The tiny, happy mice were in a race
And the Mouse ran over the Lion's face.

The Lion caught the Mouse in his big paw
And held it in front of his mighty jaw.
The Mouse looked back at the mighty Lion.
He was terrified, but he was not cryin'.

"Please, Mister Lion, I meant you no harm.
Please let me go." The Mouse said with alarm.
"If you set me free, there may come a time
When I can help you. I have done no crime."

"Ho! Ho! Ho! A runt like you can't help me.
Don't disturb my sleep, and I'll set you free."
And the released Mouse quickly ran away
Grateful to be alive another day.

It was only a few days afterward
When the mighty Lion got his reward.
In the forest, hunters had placed a net
To see what kind of big game they could get.

The big Lion was captured on the ground
Captured and wrapped, by a net, all around.
The great big Lion was a strong fighter
But his struggles just made the net tighter.

The little Mouse recognized his friend's roar.
He gathered his friends and away they tore.
The mighty Lion himself, now felt fear.
His little Mouse friend, the runt, shed a tear.

The Mouse told all his friends to form a line.
When all was set he said, "Now that's just fine.
Each of us will gnaw a piece of the twine
That the net's made of and free the feline."

In just a few moments a rent was made.
The mice stood in line, like at a parade.
The grateful Lion saluted the mice,
Stepped through the rent, and was gone in a trice.

— Carl J. Hasper

## 27

## THE LION, THE ASS AND THE FOX

A Lion, an Ass and a Fox decided to go hunting together. Luck was with them and they soon killed a fine Stag. The Lion was ravenously hungry and told the Ass to divide the carcass into three pieces so they could dine. The Ass slowly and carefully began to divide the Stag into three equal pieces, but the impatient Lion lunged at him and tore him to pieces. Then he asked the Fox to divide their prey into two pieces so they could dine together. The Fox looked at the remains of the Ass, took a tiny mouthful, and shoved the remainder to the Lion saying "Take this. Now it is divided properly." The Lion, while enjoying his meal, said to the Fox "You are very good at division. Who taught you that skill?"

"Actually", replied the Fox, looking at the remains of the Ass, "it was the Ass over there, but he doesn't know it."

MORAL: A wise person learns from the experience of others.

## THE FOX, THE ASS AND THE LION

A Fox, Ass and Lion hunted for prey
And soon a fine dead Stag, on the ground, lay.
Now the Lion's hunger was ravenous.
He told the Ass to "Divide the carcass

Into three pieces so we can all eat."
Slowly the Ass separated the meat
Into three equal pieces, carefully.
The impatient Lion seized the Ass with glee

Tore him to pieces until he was dead,
Turned to the Fox and this is what he said.
"Divide it into two pieces instead."
The Fox looked at the Ass all bloody red

Took a tiny piece for himself and said,
"Now you take the rest all bloody and red
And now it is divided properly
On that I believe we can both agree."

The Lion who was enjoying his food
And was now in a more jovial mood
Looked at the Sly Fox while the Ass yet bled
Stared at the fox and this is what he said:

"To divide without incurring my wrath
Is a great skill. Who taught you to do Math?"
"Alas. It was that dead Ass over there
But he doesn't know it, nor does he care."

— Carl J. Hasper

# 28

## THE MIGHTY OAK AND THE PUNY REED

A Mighty Oak Tree on the Bank of a River surveyed its Realm. A Storm arose and the Oak snapped in the Wind, fell into the Water, and was conveyed downstream until it came to rest amidst some Reeds near the Shore. The once Mighty Oak, amazed to see that the puny Reeds had withstood the Storm without damage, while a Mighty Oak like himself had broken, asked "Why?" A Reed replied, "You proudly resisted the thin

Air and refused to bend to its demands. We weak Reeds bowed and bent and gave it the respect it demanded."

MORAL: Pride cometh before a fall.

## THE PUNY REED AND THE MIGHTY OAK

A Mighty Oak on the Bank of a Stream
Surveyed His Realm. 'Twas a Beautiful Dream.
The God of the Wind sent a gentle Breeze
That softly caressed the Leaves of the Trees.

The Willow and Pine bent down with respect
But the arrogant Oak remained erect.
The Wind blew harder and snapped the Oak Trunk
And the Oak staggered and fell, like a Drunk.

The respectful Trees like Willow and Pine
Bent down even lower and they were fine.
Into the Stream tumbled the Mighty Oak
Because it's disrespectful Trunk was Broke.

It drifted downstream to a Shore of Reeds
Accompanied by many Acorn Seeds.
Puny Reeds, the Oak was amazed to see
Had not broken like the Trunk of a Tree.

Amazed, the Oak Tree wondered aloud, "Why?"
A Puny Reed replied, "I'll tell you why.
You disrespected the God of the Wind
And He punished you because you have sinned."

— Carl J. Hasper

# 29

## THE MILLER AND HIS SON AND THEIR ASS

A Miller decided to sell his Ass in the Marketplace. He brought his Son along so he could learn how to negotiate a sale. They marched along a country road on the way to the Market, the Miller and his Son leading their Ass. A group of boys playing at the side of the road stopped to watch the passing trio and thought it a hilarious sight. They laughed so hard it brought tears to their eyes. One of the older boys pointed at the Miller and his Son and said, "What a pair of Dummies! They have an Ass, yet do not ride it!"

The man told his Son to climb onto the Ass while

he led them, and they continued on their way. They approached a group of old men having a heated discussion at the side of the road. One of the men turned and pointed at the trio and said, "See! That's exactly what I was saying! The youth of today are pampered! He lets his Son ride the Ass while he walks!"

The Miller told his Son to dismount, and the Miller rode the Ass while his Son walked in front, leading them, and they continued on their way. They approached a group of old women having a heated discussion at the side of the road. One of the women turned and pointed at the trio saying "See! That's exactly what I was saying! Children today are abused! That man rides his Ass while his poor son struggles to keep up!"

The Miller told his Son to climb onto the Ass behind him and they continued on their way. They were nearing a Bridge which spanned a River at the edge of the town where the Marketplace was. They approached another group of people at the side of the Road. As they passed, one of them pointed at the trio and said "See! That's exactly what I was saying! There is too much animal abuse today! That big man and child are both on the back of that poor little Ass who must struggle with the heavy load! For shame! They should be carrying the poor Ass!"

The Miller and his Son dismounted. The Miller took some rope and bound the Ass's front feet together and also its back feet. He took a long sturdy pole and placed it between the front legs and back legs of the Ass.

The Miller put one end of the pole on his shoulder and told his Son to do the same with the other end of the pole. With the Ass hanging upside down, they marched on toward the bridge.

As they traversed the bridge, crowds of people stepped aside and allowed the amusing trio to pass, roaring with laughter. The Ass, feeling uncomfortable hanging upside down from the pole, and hearing the roaring laughter, began to kick at his bonds. The pole broke. The Ass tumbled onto, and over, the side of the bridge, into the river, and drowned.

MORAL:You can't please all of the People all of the time.

## THE ASS AND THE MILLER AND HIS SON

A Miller decided to sell his Ass.
He had two children, a Lad and a Lass.
He would sell his Ass in the Marketplace
In a small rural town in Thrace.

His Son, he would try to elucidate
He would teach him how to negotiate
So he took, along with his Ass, his Son.
A trip to the town would be fun.

They marched on the road to the Marketplace
The three of them walking. They did not race.
As the Miller, his Son, and the Ass strode
There were some boys at the side of the road.

The boys were laughing, with not much to do
And looked, and saw, the trio in a Queue.
They thought it was a hilarious sight
A Man, a Boy, an Ass in the Sunlight.

One of the boys pointed at the Three
And he stomped his foot, and he slapped his knee.
He laughed so hard, he had tears in his eyes.
"They have an Ass they do not utilize!"

"Climb onto the Ass." The Man told his Son.
He did not want to seem a Simpleton
And the trio continued on their way
For it was a beautiful Sunlit Day.

A group of men, at the side of the road
Was the site of their next episode.
One of the men turned, pointed, and said, "See!
Children are pampered!" He glared at the three.

"Get down off the Ass, my Son," The Man said
And the Miller climbed on the Ass instead
And the trio continued on their way
For it was a beautiful Sunlit Day.

A group of women, alongside the road
Was the site of their next episode.
"Child abuse!" one of the women cried out.
She pointed at the Miller and said, "Lout!"

"The Lad struggles to keep up while you ride!
If I were a man, I would thrash your Hide!"
"Climb up behind me." The Man told his Son.
"I am trying hard to please everyone."

And the trio continued on their way
For it was a beautiful Sunlit Day.
They were approaching a crowd near the Town
A crowd of people, each one with a frown.

"Stop Animal Abuse!" said a raised Sign.
"Get off that Donkey, you're bending its Spine!"
Said a voice, from a face, wearing a Frown
As they neared a Bridge to enter the Town.

So they both dismounted, onto the Ground.
With a Rope, the fore feet, and hind feet, were bound.
A Pole was placed between the Donkey's feet.
The two of them lifted him off the Street

And the Ass was carried high in the Air
Onto the Bridge towards the County Fair.
He was upside down, his feet in the Air
And so he struggled to get out of there.

The Pole broke, and he rolled around and round.
He fell into the Water and drowned.
Moral: If you try to please everyone
You probably will not please anyone.

— Carl J. Hasper

## *30*

## THE OLD HOUND AND HIS MASTER

A Hound who had served his Master well for many long years was losing his strength and had many age related ailments. One day while out hunting with his Master he encountered a wild Boar and seized it by the Ear but one of his teeth broke and the Boar escaped. His Master was furious and began scolding his old Hound and raised his Riding Crop and was about to strike him with it but he stopped when the old Hound said, "Master, you must know from my lifetime of service that it was not my Will nor Courage that failed me but my Strength and Teeth and I have lost them in your service." "Good boy!" said the Master to his old Hound and hugged him. When they returned home, he gave his old friend a steak dinner. The old Hound wagged his Tail.

MORAL: Noblesse Oblige: Those who have been favored by the Goddess of Fate with Fortune and Power have an obligation to help those less fortunate than themselves.

## THE MASTER AND HIS OLD HOUND

Dogs have served Mankind for thousands of Years
And shared the Sounds of the Chase with their Ears.
A Hunting Dog had served his Master well
But the Bell of age was sounding its knell.

The Master and his Hound were on a Hunt.
The old Hound's keen ears heard a Wild Boar's grunt.
The Hound pounced on the Boar and seized its Ear.
For the Boar's sharp Tusks, the Hound had no fear.

But the old Hound's Tooth broke and the Boar fled
It's only wound, the Ear, from which it bled.
The Master arrived and he was furious
And disappointed and cantankerous.

He castigated and scolded his Hound
While his sad old Hound looked up from the Ground.
He raised his Riding Crop above his Head
But stopped to listen to what his Dog said.

"Master, I've served you for many a Year
And you know that I have never shown Fear.
Neither my Will nor my Courage failed me
As I wrestled the Boar under the Tree."

"It was my Strength and Teeth that failed me
And these I have lost in my service to Thee."
"Good boy!" said the Master to his old Hound.
He hugged him and lifted him off the Ground.

That Night, for Dinner, the Hound had a Steak.
He ate so much he got a bellyache.
He slept on the Floor by his Master's Chair
Dreaming of the Chase, in the Fresh Air.

— Carl J. Hasper

# 31

## THE OLD WOMAN AND HER HEN

A poor old Woman who lived in a Hut at the edge of a Town had one egg-laying Hen. The Hen laid quality eggs that the Woman sold at a premium price. It was her only source of cash income but the Hen only laid one Egg per day. She thought to herself "If I feed my Hen twice as much Barley every day, she will lay twice as many Eggs." She tried this but, alas, the Hen became fat and so contented that she stopped laying Eggs entirely.

MORAL: Economics 101: The Law of Diminishing Returns. If one factor of production is gradually increased, output will also gradually increase, but eventually a peak output will be reached and thereafter output will decrease.

## THE HEN AND THE OLD WOMAN

An Old Woman lived at the edge of a Town.
She had one Hen for which she was renown.
But the Hen only laid one Egg a Day,
A Premium Egg she sold for Premium Pay.

Her only income, she got from the Egg.
She was so poor she almost had to beg.
"If I fed her twice as much every Day"
Thought she, "I will receive twice as much Pay."

"I'll double her Barley. I can do that."
But, alas, the Hen began to get Fat.
Fat and contented, she lays no more Eggs
And the Old Woman now goes out and begs.

— Carl J. Hasper

## *32*

## THE OX CART DRIVER AND THE SQUEAKING WHEEL

An Ox Cart had a squeaky Wheel. Annoyed, the Driver said to the Wheel "Why are you complaining? The Ox pulling us is doing all of the work and He's not complaining." They continued on for a short distance until the Wheel seized the Axle, the Axle snapped, and the Wheel fell off, whereupon the Driver and his Cargo slid off onto the side of the Road.

MORAL: A squeaking Wheel should not be cursed, but attended to.

## THE SQUEAKING WHEEL AND THE OX CART DRIVER

Long before there was a School at Oxford
Where the Thames was shallow, an Ox could ford.
Long ago, in Asia, before paved Roads
Before Wild Horses were tamed to pull Loads.

Before two-axle Wagons pulled our Loads
One-axle Ox Carts were used on our Roads
And the two-wheeled Cart was pulled by an Ox
Directed by a Driver on a Box.

Before there were Roller Bearings for Wheels
Sleeve Bearings were used and often made Squeals.
A Sleeve Bearing is a Peg in a Hole
The Peg at the end of an Axle Pole.

Inside the Hub of the Wheel was the Hole
Into which fitted the Peg on the Pole.
The Axle pressed on the rotating Wheel
And it was Friction that caused it to Squeal.

An early unknown Inventor deduced
Friction was bad and had to be reduced.
He knew something slippery was needed
And His very good advice was heeded.

Something like Wax, Fat or Vegetable Oil
Could reduce Friction and lessen the Toil.
The sliding Friction generated Heat
That could be lessened by the Fat from Meat.

Although the Sleeve Bearing was not stronger
Lubrication made it last much longer.
Not one of the Lubricants lasted long.
When the Bearing was dry, it sang its Song.

It was telling the Driver it was time
To add Lubricant. Listen to this Rhyme.
A two-wheeled Ox Cart had a Squeaking Wheel.
A Wobbly Wheel that emitted a Squeal

And the Ox Cart Driver said to the Wheel
"Why are you complaining with that loud Squeal?
It's the Ox who's doing all of the Work
And you're not doing enough Work to shirk."

The Cart continued with a Wobbly Wheel.
The Wheel continued to emit a Squeal
'Til the Axle snapped and fell to the Ground.
When the Axle snapped, you could hear the Sound.

The Wheel continued to roll 'til it fell.
Cargo tumbled into a Ditch pell mell.
The Driver landed on top of it all.
A Just Dessert for he deserved to Fall.

— Carl J. Hasper

## 33
## THE PROUD STAG

A proud Stag went to a pool to get a drink of water. The surface of the water reflected his image like a mirror and he admired his magnificent horns. But then he noticed his scrawny, skinny, unsightly legs, and was ashamed of them. He knew his legs were very useful because they enabled him to outrace his enemies. He also knew that the magnificent rack of horns was not very useful.

As he was pondering the contrast of his magnificent horns and his ugly legs, he heard the howls of an approaching pack of hounds that were helping some hunters. His ugly legs enabled him to race ahead of his pursuers and they were soon far behind, so he decided to hide in a thicket of vines and briers, but his high rack of horns became entangled and he was immobilized. The hounds caught up with him and the hunters dispatched him.

MORAL: Usefulness is more important than beauty.

## THE STAG WHO WAS PROUD

A Stag was thirsty and went to the brink
Of a pool in a glade to get a drink.
His image was reflected in the pool
And he admired it like an old fool.

He admired the horns upon his head.
"I am so handsome", to himself, he said.
His big horns were used to attract a mate
But not of much use as we shall relate.

He admired his image in the pool,
Pranced around, and strutted like an old fool.
His legs were useful. A race they could win.
But they were long, scrawny, ugly and thin.

As he looked at his ugly legs with shame
He said to himself "I'd rather be lame
If to beautiful legs I could lay claim."
But those useful legs did not deserve blame.

As the Stag stood and pondered, he heard howls
From a pack of hounds, and he heard their growls.
They were followed by hunters on horseback.
It was obvious they were on his track.

His ugly legs carried him far away
And it seemed he would live another day.
His legs had carried him, in leaps and bounds,
Far, far ahead of the pursuing hounds.

His ugly legs had a very long stride
But the Stag decided to stop and hide.
So he turned into a copse of small trees,
Vines, briers and brambles. There was no breeze.

His huge horns entangled, he thrashed about
And pulled very hard, but could not get out.
Now the hounds arrived and kept him at bay.
A shot rang out and on the ground, he lay.

— Carl J. Hasper

# 34

## THE SUN AND BOREAS

Boreas, the God of the North Wind, and the Sun were bragging about their powers, and each claimed to be more powerful than the other. Down below, a man wearing a coat was walking along a sandy beach. Boreas said to the Sun "I'll bet you I can make that man remove his coat and you cannot. That will prove which of us is more powerful." The Sun agreed.

When Boreas blew an icy blast of wind at the man, he wrapped his coat more tightly about himself, so Boreas blew even harder, and frozen spittle accompanied the strong gust of wind. The man only held tighter onto his coat so Boreas gave up.

The Sun said, "Now it is my turn." The Clouds moved out of the way and the Sun shined brightly onto the man. Soon the man was warm and began to perspire, and removed his coat and secured it around his waist using the sleeves as a belt. The Sun won the bet.

MORAL: Kindness is more persuasive than Force.

## BOREAS AND THE SUN

The Sun was arguing with Boreas,
God of the North Wind, who was an old Cuss.
Each of them claimed to have more power.
Soon the North Wind, Boreas, did glower.

It's not important to any of us
But it was to the Sun and Boreas.
Far below, a man walked along a Strand.
He wore a coat as he walked in the sand.

"Do you see that man walking down below?
I'll bet you, using the Wind that I blow,
That I can make that man remove his coat
And that you cannot." Boreas did gloat.

The Sun agreed to the test of power.
The Cold North Wind continued to glower.
When Boreas blew a blast of cold air
At the man in the coat walking down there

He raised his collar and quickened his pace
As the blast of cold air blew in his face.
A colder, stronger, gust of cold air did sing
Accompanied by spittle that did sting.

The man bowed his head as it stung his face.
He tightened his coat and quickened his pace.
The Cold North Wind continued to glower.
It seemed that he did not have the power.

So all of the clouds moved out of the way
And the bright sunshine made it a warm day.
The Sun shined so brightly upon the man
That, if he were naked, he'd get a tan.

It was not long 'til he was warm and wet
Because the heavy coat made the man sweat.
Off came the coat as down the Strand he paced.
By the sleeves, he tied it around his waist.

— Carl J. Hasper

## 35

## THE WOLF AND THE CRANE

A greedy Wolf devoured his prey ravenously. A bone got stuck in his throat. In extreme agony, he ran and howled throughout the forest. He begged any animal he met to pull out the bone. He offered a generous reward for anyone who would do so. A Crane passing by saw his plight and took pity upon him. She used her long beak to pluck the bone from the Wolf's throat.

When she asked for a reward, the Wolf bared his teeth and said, "Your reward is your life. You can boast that you were the only creature able to put your head into the jaws of a Wolf and withdraw it safely."

MORAL: Don't expect a reward when you serve the wicked. Be thankful you are not injured for your efforts.

## THE CRANE AND THE WOLF

It was hot, humid, and late in the day.
A greedy Wolf was devouring his prey.
All of a sudden a splinter of bone
Lodged in his throat and he let out a moan.

He ran and howled throughout the forest
In agony. He was sorely depressed.
He begged anyone to pull out the bone,
But all were afraid. He was all alone.

Desperately, he offered a reward.
But all were fearful. No one came forward
'Til a Crane took pity. Despite her fear,
With trepidation she gradually came near.

"If you will let me, I will try my luck.
I will use my beak, as a tool to pluck
The bone from your throat, and you will be well.
Then you can go out and again raise hell."

The Wolf looked up and opened his jaws wide
And the Crane poked her long beak deep inside.
That she could retrieve it, she had no doubt.
She grabbed hold of the bone, and pulled it out.

The grey Wolf was a most ungrateful cur.
As for the Crane's reward, he laughed at her.
"I'll reward you. Your life is your reward.
You're a tasty tidbit that I ignored.

You're lucky I did not dine on your meat.
A feathery Crane is a tasty treat.
And don't ever expect me to be kind.
Now move along before I change my mind."

— Carl J. Hasper

## *36*
## THE WOLF AND THE DOG

A skinny, hungry Wolf was wandering about late at night searching for something to eat. He met a well fed Dog and they struck up a conversation. The Wolf asked the Dog "How is it that you are so well fed while I find it difficult to find anything to eat?"

The Dog replied, "You can be just as well off as I am if you do as I do. I have a Man as a Master. I guard his property at night and every morning he rewards me by allowing me to eat the leftovers from the previous night's feast. I even get a bowl of sour beer. Follow me and perhaps you too can get a job."

As they trotted along together, the Wolf noticed a bald ring about the Dog's neck and asked about it. The Dog replied, "Oh, that's nothing. I'm very aggressive so during the daytime my Master puts a collar around my neck and chains me to a post. I sleep most of the day."

The Wolf stopped in his tracks and said "Whoa. This is as far as I go. Do you mean to tell me that you trade your freedom to do as you wish all day, and allow yourself to be chained to a post like a criminal in jail, in exchange for some leftovers from your Master's feast? I much prefer to be hungry but free. Goodbye."

MORAL: It's better to be hungry and free than a fat slave.

## THE DOG AND THE WOLF

A Wolf in the forest searched for some food.
He was hungry and not in a good mood.
As he searched in the forest late at night
He met a happy Dog in the moonlight.

They exchanged greetings and Mister Wolf said,
"How is it, Dog, that you are so well fed
While I search for food and can't find any?
That's why I am hungry, lean and skinny."

The Dog replied "You can be well fed, too.
Just listen and I'll tell you what to do.
I've a Master, whose property I guard.
I roam around all night in his big yard.

My Master stays up late and feasts at night
And he entertains guests who sometimes fight
And in the morning I get a reward
Of all the leftovers that they discard.

And sometimes I get a bowl of sour beer
For which I have become too fond, I fear.
Maybe you can get a job to help me.
Follow me to my Master and we'll see."

As they walked, and Dog explained everything,
The Wolf saw, around the Dog's neck, a ring.
'Twas a ring that was bald and had no hair.
And so he asked the Dog "What is that there?"

The Dog replied, "It is a small matter
So we can wait and discuss it later."
The Wolf replied, "No. I want to know now."
The Dog said, "To your wishes I will bow.

I am aggressive so during the day
They collar me so I can't run away.
They put a collar 'round my neck all day
And chain me so I can not run away."

They chain me to a post the entire day
But I don't care, I'm sleeping anyway."
Mister wolf stopped in his tracks and said, "Whoa."
He told Dog "This is as far as I go.

You trade your freedom to do as you wish
For stale scraps and bones and beer in a dish?
No thanks! I much prefer to be hungry
Lean and skinny so long as I am free."

— Carl J. Hasper

## 37

## THE WOLF AND THE LAMB

A hungry Wolf was drinking water from a small stream. He looked downstream and saw a little Lamb munching grass at the edge of the stream. He decided she was to be his dinner. The Wolf, as many of us also do, decided to rationalize his act. He wanted to justify what he was about to do to the poor defenseless Lamb. As he approached her, he said "Hey! I'm trying to get a drink of clean water, and you are making it all muddy!" Startled, the little Lamb politely replied, "But Mr. Wolf, I am downstream from you. Even if I muddy the water, which I am not because I am at the side of the stream and not in it, the muddy water would flow away from you." The Wolf continued his approach and replied, "That may be so, but I remember that it was you who made fun of me last year, and laughed at me." The little Lamb replied, "But Mr. Wolf, I'm only three months old. I was not yet born last year." The Wolf pounced upon the defenseless little Lamb saying "Then it must have been your mother. It's all the same to me. I'm Hungry."

MORAL: If you are weak it is futile to reason with a strong bully.

## THE LAMB AND THE WOLF

A Wolf was drinking water from a stream.
He was hungry and his eyes had no gleam.
Downstream, he saw a small Lamb munching grass.
"I'll not let this opportunity pass"

Said the Wolf to himself. "I'll go nearer
And talk as I approach closer to her."
As the crafty wolf approached her he said
"Hey You!" The little Lamb raised up her head.

"You are making the water all muddy!
I want to drink clean water, not cruddy."
Fearfully, the wee little Lamb replied
"But Mr. Wolf" with her eyes very wide

"But Mr. Wolf, I am downstream from you
If you look closely, it's as clear as new."
The Wolf continued his approach and said
"Even if so, I am still seeing red.

I remember it was you who made fun
Of me last year. I wished I had a gun."
"But Mr. Wolf I'm only three months old,
Not yet born last year, and never that bold."

The Wolf pounced upon the defenseless Lamb
Saying "It's too bad. I don't give a damn.
I'm good at excuses. Here's another.
It must have been your father or mother."

— Carl J. Hasper

# 38

# THE WOODSMAN AND THE TREES

A Woodsman needed a handle for his ax. He entered the forest and asked the trees to give him some wood for a handle. To the big, strong trees such as the mighty Oak, the Cedar, and the Elm, this seemed a reasonable request, and so they declared that a plain simple Ash tree should provide the wood the man needed.

The man shaped the wood and fitted it into his ax head. Then he proceeded to chop down the magnificent trees in the forest.

It was not long before the big strong trees,

observing the woodsman's approach and destruction, realized their folly. The mighty Oak, much like the talking Oak of Dordona, of ancient Greek mythology, was able to speak, and had oracular powers. He said to his neighbors, the mighty Cedar and Elm, "If only we had been more careful and not sacrificed our little brother, the Ash, we would not be in the predicament we find ourselves in now."

MORAL 1: When the strong surrender the rights of the weak, they create a handle that can be used to pry away their own rights.

MORAL 2: Stand together as one or all will fall one-by-one.

MORAL 3: The strong must support the weak or the strong will lose their own rights.

## THE TREES AND THE WOODSMAN

There once was a Forest on a mountain.
It was green and even had a fountain.
It was pristine and everything was green.
Trees are beautiful and good. They're not mean.

A Woodsman entered the Forest in quest
Of an ax handle and made a request.
Boldly he walked towards the big stately trees
While caressed by a gently blowing breeze.

"I need wood for a handle, if you please."
He made the request to the great big trees.
He did not demand, he did not act tough.
The request seemed reasonable enough.

The Oak, the Cedar, and Elm then discussed
The request from the man whom they did trust.
They discussed it and decided "Why not?
After all, he's not asking for a lot.

Take a piece from that small Ash" they told him.
"But do not take the trunk, only a limb."
They did not consult the small Ash at all.
And therein lies the reason for their fall.

The Woodsman took it, and shaped it with skill
Without concern for the wood he did kill.
It fit perfectly into his ax head.
He had no concern for the wood was dead.

He chopped a tree here. And he chopped one there.
He chopped the trees down almost everywhere.
The big trees observed his approach with fear.
And thought "It won't be long and he'll be here!"

But they could do nothing. It was too late.
The little Ash said, "You deserve your fate!"

— Carl J. Hasper

# 39
## TWO TRAVELERS AND A BEAR

Two strangers met at the edge of a forest that was known to be dangerous. Before proceeding along the road through the forest, they agreed that if either of them was attacked, by man or beast, the other would come to his assistance.

They had only gone a short distance when they were charged by a huge bear. One of the men, fast and agile, climbed a tree in terror. The other man, not so fast or agile, fell prone on the ground and pretended to be dead. The bear ambled over to him and sniffed him and looked him over. Thinking the man was dead, and not having seen where the other man had gone, the bear walked away into the forest.

Both of the men, fearing the bear might return, remained where they were for some time. When satisfied the bear had gone away, the man got up off the ground and the other man descended from the tree and came over to him. With a big grin on his face he asked, "Tell me, friend, what did that bear say to you? I noticed he put his nose to your ear. He must have said something."

"Why yes, as a matter of fact, he did," he replied. "He told me never to trust a cowardly stranger like you to assist me."

MORAL: Don't trust strangers.

## A BEAR AND TWO TRAVELERS

A forest that was known for its dangers
Long ago, was not patrolled by Rangers.
At the forest's edge, where two strangers met
Said one to the other "Tut, tut. Don't fret."

"If we both team up we will have more clout
And we should have less to worry about."
Two strangers had met at the forest's edge
And both of them made a most solemn pledge.

"If I am attacked, you come to my aid.
You do the same in case we are waylaid."
They had not gone far and the day was fair
When they were charged by a huge furry bear.

One man, fast and agile, climbed up a tree
And then looked down to see what he could see.
The other man, slower, fell to the ground
And he played dead and did not make a sound.

The bear sniffed at the terrified man's ear
The man who was prone, and stricken with fear.
The bear sniffed him and then rolled him over.
The bear rolled him over in the clover.

Thinking the man dead, the bear walked away.
The terrified man continued to pray.
In the clover he continued to lay
'Til he was sure the bear had gone away.

The terrified man got up from the ground
And then he carefully looked all around.
The forest was quiet. There was no sound
And the other man climbed down to the ground.

The man from the tree, with a smile of glee
Came over and said "Will you please tell me
What that bear said as I watched from the tree?
I hope you will share the secret with me."

"As a matter of fact, that bear was wise.
He said to me as he looked in my eyes
Never to trust a cowardly stranger
When ever I'm confronted with danger."

— Carl J. Hasper

# 40

## ZEUS AND THE HONEYBEE

In Ancient Times, Aeons ago, a Honeybee had a bountiful Harvest and her Honeycombs were overflowing with the Mellifluous Fluid, so she decided to fly up to Olympus and present Zeus with some of her Honey in thanks for the Bounteous Harvest. Zeus was so pleased with the gift that he promised to grant her whatever she wished. "Thank you Glorious Zeus. I would be pleased if you would grant your humble servants a Sting so that if anyone tries to steal our Honey, we can use a fatal Sting that will kill."

Zeus loved mankind and was angry with her request for such a severe punishment for Theft, yet he was obligated to grant it. Zeus replied, "I will grant your Wish, but probably not as you desired. You shall have a fatal Sting. If anyone tries to steal your Honey, you may sting him, and it will hurt him, but it will be fatal to you."

MORAL 1: The punishment should fit the Crime.

MORAL 2: Be careful what you wish for.

## THE HONEYBEE AND ZEUS

Aeons ago there was a Honeybee
In a Meadow near the Aegean Sea.
In the Spring and in the Summer and Fall
Were Flowers with enough Honey for all.

Flowers with Petals, every Shape and Size
Wondrous Beauty to behold with one's Eyes.
There were Aromas with wondrous Fragrance
To titillate the Olfactory Sense.

It was a Garden of Eden for Bees.
They hurried about in a Gentle Breeze.
One year there was a bounteous Harvest.
Much Nectar was brought back to the Bee's Nest.

The Honeybees brought back Load after Load.
The Mellifluous Fluid overflowed.
A Bee decided to give thanks to Zeus
For the Bounteous Harvest of the Juice.

There were no Clouds, and the Day was sunny
As she flew to Olympus with Honey.
Olympus was the Home of the God Zeus
And she wanted to thank Him for the Juice.

"Thank you, Dear Zeus, for the Nectar you give
Delicious Nectar that we need to live.
Here's some Honey we made with the Nectar.
I have brought it a long way, from afar."

Zeus, pleased with the gift, said to the Bee
"It's not often that Bees bring Gifts to me.
Most often they come to beg and plea.
I'm happy to have met you, little Bee.

Thanks. Now I'd like to grant a Wish for you.
Tell me your Wish and I'll make it come true."
"I wish to have a Sting for every Bee
So we can protect, from theft, our Honey."

To have a Sting that's Lethal and will kill
Would give, to each one of us Bees, a thrill."
Now Zeus was not happy with this request.
For Justice from the Gods, it was a Test.

I must be careful what I grant this Bee
Or I will regret it and be sorry.
To Kill is just another form of theft.
The victim, of Life itself, is bereft.

Death is too great a punishment for Theft
So in granting this Wish I must be deft.
"I'll grant a fatal Sting to Honeybees
And your outrage, at Theft, it may appease

But my Gift, to Bees, I think will displease.
Its use will be Fatal to Honeybees."

— Carl Hasper

# About the Author

Carl J. Hasper

The author was born in Foley, Alabama, on October 20, 1936. He began school in a two-room Catholic school in Elberta, Alabama, when five years of age, and daydreamed his way through eight different schools in Alabama and Illinois, finally graduating at seventeen from a public high school in Harvey, Illinois. He enlisted in the US Navy when seventeen years of age. It was a "kiddie cruise" and required parental approval. He would be released from active duty when he reached the age of twenty-one. He graduated from the US Navy Electronics School on Treasure Island in San Francisco Bay.

He served aboard LSTs as an Electronics Technician, radar specialist, and was honorably discharged as a second class petty officer just before he was twenty-one years old. While in the Navy, he enrolled in a correspondence course to study radio and television engineering in preparation for taking the FCC examination to obtain a Radiotelephone Operator's license needed to work as a Radio or TV station engineer. He passed the exam and obtained the license, with a Radar endorsement. Jobs were scarce because Radio and TV shows were now being pre-recorded on magnetic tape and not as many engineers were needed as had been required for "live" shows.

He obtained a job for a major US Airline at LaGuardia Airport as a radio mechanic, which required the same FCC license. He worked on the midnight shift, and enrolled in Queens College, where he studied pre-engineering, and graduated from City College in New York City with a baccalaureate in Electrical Engineering. He met Barbara, his wife-to-be, when she was completing her studies at Queens College for a baccalaureate in Mathematics to become a mathematics teacher.

They have one child, Marianne, who lives nearby. He is yet married to Barbara, over fifty-five years later. They live in the same house they purchased in 1965, over fifty years ago. He retired from the airline twenty years ago. About seven years ago, he acquired a passion for writing rhymed poetry. It is a pleasant disease.

28312881R00097

Made in the USA
Middletown, DE
10 January 2016